The Book of Shores

Mary Buchinger

LILY POETRY REVIEW BOOKS

for Steve, Liam, Kai

Contents

Full sail, I voyage over the boundless ocean,
and I tell you nothing is permanent in all the world.
All things are fluent; every image forms,
wandering through change. Time is itself a river
in constant movement, and the hours flow by
like water, wave on wave, pursued and pursuing,
forever fugitive, forever new

Ovid, *Metamorphoses*

I am the shore and the ocean, awaiting myself on both sides.

Dejan Stojanović, *The Shape*

Love is a shore

It needs shoring up   forms
of love have ways of
shaping and reshaping   being
shaped and reshaped
waves of love
upon rock of love   grains of
love   like sand   like salt
body of love
    How strange to be
at once a fragment and
a whole
There's no sense in this   no logic
here   upon this shore

Hilary Sallick, *love is a shore*

Seaway

Constant the movement away
or toward   watery self flows
laps at the door   the engineered
lock snaps shut

    (what is created by humans
        is almost always alien)

floating cumulus snags
  the upper branches
  of an invisible tree
   and ribbons the sky

                  [how
I descend the ladder
without shoes, trying not to slip,
rungs pressing into the arches
of my feet,

   while, far below,
students wait, expectant, for my
lecture

     when I arrive at the bottom,
all my knowledge is
beyond my reach
        formless as the earth
        on that first day]

A clear jar of water anchors the tablecloth
its glass a solidish liquid of sand + heat

its water trembles as I write registers
the quake of my words

~

In day-sleep
I seek an upstream
    a fresh new other

(how to make sense
of where I am)

  baby in a bulrush basket
  waves at the reeds

                where is the finder?

White deck chairs bear the dead home

~

The streaming and bifurcating
  blue shows me what to do

      I find my way
    in the coast of you

  everything that is loved
              becomes solid and directional

~

How tiresome the torrent

the screed of water
  insists by its presence
on a ground to absorb it
  seeks what can be washed
    and washed away

I don't know if this is how I am loved
and how I love

it's what gives life and what frees it

          ~

          [when I reach the bottom of the ladder
                              I have no idea
                              what to say

    all I've ever known has turned shapeless

                    I find myself going
                    back to the beginning—

A phoneme I tell the students
is the smallest
piece of meaning

              the building block of language
they show no interest

          my words
          hold no relevance]

  surely tributaries feel this too

    ~

Every day methadone mile is there
corrupt sidewalk corrugated cardboard
cushions the cracks

here a child   mother within without
what it is to become self-uncontained

I don't live here my mind does

     [two men sidle up, one at each elbow
          you are being watched they tell me]

observer witness voyeur
what is human curiosity?

          [*your watching will be curtailed* they tell me]

how seeing is: one third inside
one third out, the rest brackish

     yet the eye is owned and resides

          ~

My neighbor has an eye
that never shuts
trained on her porch
it sees without agency

     I didn't know I was
     watched when I hid
     her packages from

street view   arranging
her pots of flowers
to hide the goods
from those who
roam the streets
with a trunk to fill

my worry caught
in the motion of me
in her digital eye

(Who is looking
in the seeway?)

ocean of vision
flotsam & jetsam
that someone let go
into the stream

(what was that dream?)

~

The limits of foresight—

I scramble in the shadowlands
what could have been discerned
(some did see and say) was inconvenient

the prophets raise their heads
and lose them

I scuttle I scurry
the fire it sees me

~

The birds know the currents
    wear them inside like intestines
a magnetized stone between the eyes
        tells them where to go

They ride waves they feel
 and catch   seeing with the body
    and change with their flight
the course of those who follow

~

The sculpture in my city square
orbits eyeless in the air

    three spinning metal boats
     sail the wind invite me
    to dizzy-see an ocean-sky

~

[Outside on a platform
we are naked together

I raise my body over him
my perfect breast in
his perfect mouth—

then we pause (he has to
fill a work order)

as I wait, I count his remotes,
six, lined up on the railing—

my manager of light]

     ~

Once I recorded the light
and ran out of words

I was flying over the earth
in a 737
        the airy geography
slipping and falling beside me

   nets and knots of cloud and sky
      figment and fragment—

I tried to write what I saw
it was like (something) I wrote

but already that was wrong
the light is like nothing

     ~

I dreamt we motored along
in our boat we were a whole family
carefree and joyful as an island nation

the ocean a deeper blue
the sky too had begun to deepen
when we realized we'd lost track
of the continent   uneven masses
darkened the horizon   we tried
to decipher them

                    then a boat
big as a farmhouse appeared
with lit mullioned windows

was it heading out or in?
we attached ourselves
if only not to be lost alone

                    ⌐

My friend said she was
lying in bed with mortality
beside her

              she was curious
      let mortality touch her

she too reached out
      ran her fingers
            along its surface

                  mortality rippled
      like water

                  then grew
      tender
            as a ripened fruit

In the *fulness of time:*

   stones stacked
one by one
   across a rivulet
        recruitment
of sticks and mud

what small hands
can find

     for whole
moments
      the water
seems baffled
     halting

  as it builds up
steady
   against the pieced-
   together dam

Island

•

The iris makes an island
of the pupil of my eye

two islands afloat
make an island of me

•

Weak watery eyes, he said,
it runs in your family

(even the word 'family'
makes me cry)

•

island: that which is
perceived to be
surrounded by
something other

different from
(isolated, detached)

•

In my dream   a naked woman
sits on the floor of a stage
in a filled auditorium

I watch as she lowers her head toward her chest
her sheath of black hair falls straight
down her scarred bronze back

She draws her knees toward her breasts
the large loaves folding somehow inside

Then a forest-green leaf forms around her
rising up it covers her like a jack-in-the-pulpit

Her entire body podded   the flesh of her
gone from view   safe somewhere deep
within the verdant blanket

•

What is refuge
but *inside*

shelter from
outside

•

The cat
bridges my thighs

   legs and tail tucked
   her compact coil
   thrums with warmth

   •

What happiness
passes the test

   jumps the little
   ship of self?

   •

    North of the hamlet
    the garbage heap grew
    hauled in wheelbarrows
    from each household
    until hamlet and heap
    merged into one

   •

(I scratch words
inside the cat on my page

how safe they feel
in the outline of her fur—

Look! her sketched ears
cocked above my scribble)

•

There is always more
than you can see

each something
presents another
possibility

lamb in the grass
lamb on the plate

•

Aunt Marie wanted
a classic horse-head
hitching post
on the homestead
where my father was born
on the second floor

She had no horses
she'd lost her first
husband and son
suddenly and young

My uncle said *No*
we don't need
no hitching post

She found a replica
in a catalogue
paid the $72
plus shipping and
dug a hole
between house and garage

Each late spring
she planted
geraniums red as
a horse's mouth
beneath the islanded
iron ring

•

Poison ivy rings Fresh Pond

•

a moat separates self
from self   self from other

what is first a formal distance
may grow unbridgeable

unmoored personhood

contract and clauses
abandoned

                        •

                is vs. *isn't*
        mutual uprising

                a lake
              is a kind
              of island

                •

Once I tried to read the clouds, then I realized
we didn't share a language. I found myself relying
on what I already knew— objects, emotions.

The clouds said, that's okay, you have to start somewhere.
And then, the clouds began to read me.

                •

I drifted
like a dead star
and looked down
on the earth

which had become a grey plank
balancing
just so
upon a grey cylinder

I calculated
what was required
for the earth-plank

to not tip   not fall
this way   or   that way

the exact centers
of each
aligning
exactly

•

I try to shield it   cup my hands

around it   feed it it's so thin

tenuous   shadowlike

it can do things   can teach me

but it's needy and sometimes I

stray from it or squander it

or overwhelm it   I get hungry

tired out I forget who I belong to

•

In winter   the cats abandon
the sun porch when morning turns
afternoon   they follow the sun
into other rooms

•

This morning as I was about to pour
    hot water from the kettle into my mug
a large tawny spider the same color as my skin
crawled out from the sleeve of my robe
    and onto my wrist

We surprised each other—
        startled into awareness

Peninsula

;

Ear projects from skull
skull from neck

      my eyes on a stalk
assemble a whole
inside and out

        A word
lifts from lexicon
bee from hive

          Held, a peninsula juts
  jaunty into straits

My love, a cold-frilled bluff

   ;

You and I cooccur
that connects me
to you

    makes us part
of one another and of
something other

the peninsular landscape
  is algebra   is synecdoche

   ;

....the bees receive
very many influences
from the starry worlds...

When one stands
before a hive of bees
*   one should say*
* quite solemnly to oneself:*

*   "By way of the bee-hive*
* the whole Cosmos enters [me]*
and makes [me] strong and able."

                ;

The *thing-in-itself*
                        substratum of all appearances

        from which you and I spring—

                ;

Voluptuous lions
gambol on my lawn

each grips the neck
of the other
    with its ivory claws

detects the pulse
that could end its own

;

My dog finds the length of her leash
  my body holds her

the world of the trail the sky
    the bushes surrounds us   confirms
      her relation to me   She is my

idea   no, my stomach
      and eyes   at the end
          of a retractable leash

;

What magnitude of belonging
                what measure?

;

The gun is a peninsula
extending from a hot or cold emotion

it charges all that surrounds   brandished
cancellation   its continent grows
with its colonies   how iron heats up
when struck and can be simply useful

;

Within the bedroom of the fens
          a man a woman argue

You!
          No, you!

                    the reed walls sway
seed-heads purple and bristle

          ;

Just above the winter
surface of the reservoir

          a tree branch dangles

   wind and cold conspire
     dip the limb
freeze the drops
     again again

          form a glass
          tent of ice

a kind of shelter

     entangled story
     hardened   held
     till spring

;

Boston's Back Bay sinks
and a street in Stockholm
        rises rebounding still
    from the melted weight
      of the last Ice Age

;

Hoisted
high on someone's shoulders
        and carried all around

    I watch others chase a ball
below me on the grassy meadow
I see so much from up here

You're so tall! I exclaim, and in that moment
        wonder, am I getting too heavy,
and, how in the world
        will I ever get down?

;

The semi-colon says something more is coming

    some attached part, or qualification;

Parts, it says, are what make this Whole

My student has　⁏　in blue-black
tattooed on the pulse of her wrist

   it signifies a decision was made
      to *not end*

I teach within her deliberate pause

   an independent clause

    ;

Theory & Practice of Self:

Last night I found myself
in the hospital
needing help

   When finally I'm called
   into an examination room
   someone wheels in my father

   He is shrunken & mute

   The Doctor looks at him
   & at me
      tries to figure out
   who needs attention

Me I tell the Doctor

   My father is here & not really here

A Doctor can do nothing for him

     Next they bring in a swaddled baby
for me to nurse

With the baby latched on my breast
I try to explain why I'm here

The Doctor wants to attend to the baby
but I know the baby is fine

I am the one who needs care

    Still, it's a dream,
 everyone in it is me
I must learn
to listen

    ;

Trash strewn on the path in the fens
      bag-scraps   a litter of wet
  plastic puddles unseeping

Bic lighters neon green & hot pink
   a clear clamshell full of ginger cookies
      not yet discovered by any mouth

 A picnic of forks broken
at the intersection of paths
   indigestible fodder

    ;

Speculative Futurism Unmoored

1. Root cause analysis (applying <u>The 5 Whys</u>)

    TOPIC: Humans are Destroying the Earth

2. Why?

    Because humans need to live

3. Why?

    Do you mean, why does humans' need to live destroy the earth?

    or, why do humans need to live?

    Please clarify.

Recalculating.

;

My dog's nails click on the floor
down the hall in the night
    each click a flash of gold light:
        this too left undone

;

After viewing an exhibit
   of Dutch interiors I dream
I have to tear off the ear
   of the girl who is with me
so she can fit through the window
   we are desperate to climb into

   We gaze inside the kitchen—
pots pans ladles dangle from hooks
   and just beyond, a room
         that opens into a room
   that opens into a sunlit courtyard—
         we must get inside!

So I take the girl's ear
   and rip it in half

   She doesn't cry out
the ear doesn't bleed

What now? Clean it?
   Sew it back on?

In horror I wake   wanting
   to go back   tell the girl
   the scar will be a key

   her ear in my palm—
      a courtyard
   flushed with light

;

One platter of images after another
smashes at my feet   I carry the shards
    in hands I do not recognize

;

There's been something of the divine
in our correspondence, my friend writes

and I know what my friend means—

the delicate sepia images transmitted between us
    (winter mulberries, fallow fields, the trunk of an elm)

and the wisdom, each word
    like a handful of grain
        in a horse's bucket

I feel nourished and in my friend's debt—
        so little I've given in return

But, my friend writes, *this will be my last letter*
        We've run out of God

;

I extend   into a space   of other
    like a flame on a candle

        the jutting jaunty

      believing I'm held
a part of some whole

        the air itself
            feeds
          flicks
      my fire

Archipelago

...

dregs at the bottom
  of the continent

   crumbs
 to be swept
from the map

(broken mirror on the sidewalk
  its splinters dazzled by sun

     an accident   this beauty
wreckage   wrought

                  the sky fills in

            each fragment brims)

    an *archipelago*:

a chain of islands

      and also,

what contains them—

Tierra del Fuego—
                    sparks
                  flung across
                     the Strait

...

The poet canceled
the place where she grew up

where she gave birth to her children
and raised them

Sometimes I too feel ready
to excise and renew

I bite my nails
trim the split ends of my hair

I think about the things
that will be gone
how they will leave me

...

The flowers from my friend
lean out from a cut-glass vase
that cuts their stems
into diamonds of green

The cat chews
on the single stalk
of purple buds

...

When I was a child
      one of my chores
            was to watch over
          the burn barrel

poke the blaze
  help the fire turn the pages
      of the Sears catalogue
        its socks and small houses

and render its complete world of things
  to flame and ash

I loved to watch the grey elements
       played by wind and oxidation

       twirl up and away
           littering the sky

     then fall cool
         into the garden

    …

   I recognize my archipelago

  the self in pieces some semblance

of what was

   pure floating of incorrigible bits

      un-summing

a missing of the homeland

(that indelible idea)

...

In the small hour
of writing at the table
in my dining room
my coffee chills

and the phone lights up
makes a nudging noise
the smallest *ding* to let me know
it's alive with people and news

each little question niggles
till finally I surrender my pencil
allow myself to be pulled away
in relation to another

neither of us can see who we
are addressing or what light
surrounds the other   what soft
insistent jazz or distraction

and the hour parts from itself

...

The flowers from my friend
  I can't bear to toss them
drop petal then petal
   this way and that

their only tune is time
what separates them from their stem
as they proceed from glory
into glory   an ecclesiastical
hymn I too hum

...

The table holds

islands of placemats salt-cellar

candles that wait

things I can map

...

I ferry books to and fro
in my backpack

read one and then another

some of the words
lodge in my head

join with others
make a sort of shape
possible affinities

sometimes I sense other shores

...

The archipelago is

   the thrift shop of land forms

      crowd-funded geography

         pocket change

shiny bits strewn about—

   remnants of a great lecture

      of a well-conceived meal

     of a lineage

   ...

Something built, say a republic,
with principles and laws, a constitution
imperfect but mostly solid—

 it too can be chipped away   divided

  it is the wall of Uruk
 Gilgamesh walked along it
knew to inspect the ramparts
conservation of the built thing
    his legacy

Time is a weather
   the good an effort
        an active plan
      and plaster

What I take for granted,
   that very thing imperiled

      ...

   —the body, for instance
I inhabit daily

   it is mostly the same
as I remember it
from night to morning
      again and again

   yet it changes utterly
becomes strange to me
even as it remains familiar

   inside is the undoing

each piece of the whole
having left the original
   meeting place
                     unspools
   from its beginnings
            in the ways allowed it

revealing as it goes
   what's been fostered
   nurtured neglected

   I wake to the history
of my body, each day
another jotting

...

What is Cassiopeia
but an archipelago of light
lassoed by a name?

...

I used to think
   you and I floated together

buoyed by something shared
      as we trundled about
      the permanent fact
      of the continent

but I see now we're treading water
      as you gaze off into one distance
      and I into another

   our views of what
holds us here distinct
   and unrelated

...

Once
   a body of water
revealed itself to me
   as an eternal truth

The silvery water
concealed reflected
reeds flashing entities
slippery things that
do not drown

until
captured   spent
they floated
to the surface—

glittering fragments
of a distant sun

...

Rain separates the branches
of the slightly-orange false cypress

between its sodden limbs small windows
sparrows whirr through

...

The landscape of the archipelago
is loss   memory   dream
something that once was—

deer tracks
across a snowy field

                each impression
                        a mark
            of movement
                            (hoof
                    blood hunger)

            ...

Crossing an arid border
    between two countries
        in South America
                I waited in line
        blue passport in hand

In the corner of the room
            was a glass box
                and in the box
    a small mummified human

its skin the color of a cured cigar

            it curled into itself
        but somehow its eyes
        the place where its eyes used to be
    found a way
            to seem to look at me

            ...

Once there was a continent
        I belonged to

What you seek
is what you find
because it is
already in you
as an image

...

I canoed a sinuous river
  with a storybook forest on its banks

    my passage was slow and deliberate
      guided by the current

    then I saw below my vessel
the tarnished armor of a turtle

its clawed legs scratched the water
  as it urged itself into the depths

and as I watched I could see more
   turtles   down and down they swam

  the domes of them disappearing
one by one beneath the visible realm

...

  Three poets sit in chairs
  at the front of the room
  awaiting their turn to read

...

Within me
is a record

a memory of rising
    from the ocean of my mother:

I clambered through a chute
        and emerged on a cliff

  to my right was a perilous drop
    the rocks below splotched
        white brown   red
        amnion   meconium
      a kind of trail

to my left I saw a lighted cottage
and heard laughter
singing
      a shore

Strait

[space between]
[neither here nor there]

                / /

should've spoken to her

felt unworthy of her grief
unkempt unclean

unready to accept what she had to offer
unable to extend what she surely needed

in that public space   filled with others
I climbed the stairs away from her

                / /

A necklace
curled like a silver snake
between cobblestones

its chain knotted
its tiny heart scraped
and scratched
   lost by someone
   warms in my hand

its concentrated
weight lodges
in the linty corner
of my winter jacket

/ /

I enter the rain
and follow a young child
into the crosswalk
his umbrella threatens
to kite him away

his father strides ahead
unconcerned
does not look back

I carry the worry for him
shepherd the child and his umbrella
across the lanes of the Avenue

/ /

the dog goes out
sniffs and pees

then returns from
the outside world
its cornucopia of odors
its gutter treats

and finds me at my desk
presses the cold
 of her fur against my leg

  she tells me she is here
she has been away
doing dog things
  in a different world

      the rug at my feet
        her other dream

        [ ]

[captive]
[cramped]

        / /

Brother, I have to stop writing
because the page is only getting smaller
and I remain,

        / /

      An active-shooter alert
          rings my phone

and I imagine now
the scene at the hospital
down the street

nurses and doctors in scrubs
sheltering in some prescribed place

patients learning of a new way
they could die in a clean well-lit room

/ /

when I was young   pheasants jeweled
the narrow rows between dried cornstalks

and I was sent into the field to find
the birds huddled in quiet community

to scare them with my voice and small body
flush their beauty toward the guns

/ /

the prettiest sandals
I ever wore
had wood-veneer heels
and thin maroon straps
that drew blood
when I danced

/ /

One night my son and I
        found ourselves
    in the air

        gripping
    a thin metal bar

        our feet perched
      barely   on a rung

      we could have been birds
    but we felt paralyzed   powerless

    we had to move forward
        so little to go on

        / /

All straits,
and none but straits…

        [ ]

[channel, passage]
[and then]

/ /

an envelope full of trees
was mailed across the sea

Gift it said Three black-
stroked trees   spritzed
with silver   honey-gold
halo of bees DO NOT
BEND   The parable
of the willow   met
its west

        and just before
winter too

/ /

I tamed a feral cat when I was a child
she spat and hissed whenever I drew near
        we were terrified of each other

    but she looked so soft   angora cream
    and ginger unlike any other barn cat
        I wanted to pet her
            to hold her

Her hunger broke her spirit
    no her spirit changed as she came
    to eat the food I put out for her

each day a little closer to me
until finally she was mine
more mine than any cat
has ever been

I named her *mein Schatz*
my Treasure

/ /

speaking outside of my self
my mother tongue sometimes foreign

the strait of translation

from one language to another
feeling into word

This is true: a tree is made of air

[ ]

[currents]
[visible and invisible]

/ /

I couldn't have known
where now my house
was once a river

the loamy bed
slack-jawed peat
swells and caves

the sundry calamitous
contingencies
a season can reveal

/ /

When it's icy, walk like a penguin
says my mother, nearly ninety

She demonstrates in the kitchen
her weight shifting forward
onto her sturdy black shoe

/ /

I can do this, I say

I cast a thought from here to there
reel myself over its thread

It was first imagined
then I was bodily there

/ /

Mid-recital at Memorial Chapel
a woman in the pew in front of me
      gets up and leaves
        scarf pulled across her face
      she rushes down the aisle

Buxtehude organ notes slather the air
        search for conclusion
      the stranger's sudden departure
      changes what I hear

/ /

I'm lost, he didn't say
his silence filling me

/ /

    everyday straits—
the blue wall of my room
      my little yard
      the stone path
      between houses

/ /

The man beside me says
  This is where the shipyard once was

  They built ocean-bound Antelope clippers
  here on the banks of the Mystic

I move the word swiftly
      across my tongue *MissiTuk—*

    what once brackish
  swelled its banks

    now sliced from ocean
    fresh tamed trashed

years days minutes surge
upthrough skin that gives

        / /

(INLAND)

In INLAND
   (in the _Inn of In_)

  reside the deepest greens
the darkest forest of inside

What's in there? you ask
   again & again

Looking for what?

Neither of us can decide

   still you keep rooting around

     Ø

if not Shore—

    that edge of
heaving & new

   with stakes of herons
stately in ebbtide

lively spinning
     of minnow

    the not-rot
of borderland

 where rushes of marsh
merge
   submerge

pocked green
   beds come go

     o watery depths!
  the sucking mud—

then

    INLAND
         in amber

(what is*n't* & was*n't* & wo*n't*)

    Ø

threshold foothold toe-
         finger- choke-
            hold

    Ø

Even INLAND
  was once a sea—

    a shallow sea that turned
  the living to limestone

      an ankle-deep sea
      of economy

   a shiny miry
    mirror
    of sun

Ø

But, what's inside? you ask

Which catalog shall I reach for—
        the Living, or the Dead?

There are twisted things—
            chain coral & pincushion & petoskey

        imprints & exprints

there is what was left
when the sun was overhead—

the smallest of shadows
        that grew & grew

        Ø

& there once was a self
 known only to self

who carried the sea
wherever she went—

    skirt of water
    piney shawl

she loved the creatures dead in their shells
she plucked & pickled them
broke & built with them

paneled her house with the dead
white of the shells

Ø

How are your dead? I ask
when it's quiet

    & I've forgotten
    where I am

Ø

the shoreless interior
an airless place
of no coming no going

a skiffless wilderness

stillborn moon
    vast unknown

incubator
    of storm & misdirection

Ø

& here you are
requesting a map
texture you call it

the ups & downs
of topography
    squirrely lines
        tell the relief

in truth
　　what you seek
are sinkholes & swamps

the River that runs through

　Ø

Grab your fishing pole!
　Let out some line

String your bow
fletch your arrow—

　but the wild you seek
　　is not what lives
　　　in INLAND

(the Prairie long-ago walled
　the Sky contrailed)

belt of rust
& belly of stars

　Ø

Plato was inside
　& outside of
INLAND's cave

We know Everything
Everything is known
　remember?

Ø

the skull of the moose
 its white machinery
  of ovals and holes
 emerges from dirt

like a dentist I pick
 at its teeth   test
  their hold
in the mandible

  tap each one
canine   incisor
 rattle their marble

 I imagine a pair of them
in my pocket
 knocking anew

but the clean ivory
       gumdrops
    wedged in bone
  do not yield
   to my hand

the long loop of jaw
 signature of its species
        presses soundless
  into the ground

 remnants of horns
spread ear-shaped in air
 (the great chandeliers
      missing)

I trace with my finger
  the cup & curve
  of zygomatic arch

  all the meaningful
    spaces here
    are blank

to look into this moose's eyes
I'd have to enter the earth—
    that other INLAND
    ; the after-birth

        Ø

    A diffusion of light
        catches my eye—

a dead limb
    & live low bushes
  encased in airy aspic

    yellow grasses
        a haloed glow!—

what I saw from that side
disappears from over here

I approach
  looking for what I remember

    & *Ah!*

           a grass spider
waits upside down
      inside its tent

I breathe & watch
      the gossamer shudders

           Ø

In INLAND
           you can believe
there's no shore

      that you see
      what there is
& there is no more

the Carnival outside
the unreal that reels beyond

      is an unknowable other
      a deathbed
      a poem

           Ø

      INLAND
everyone is aghast
      I mean, a guest

Can't I live there too? you ask
Not even I do I answer

its tundra its barrens
flatlands flatline

fill & flip
with windmills
& ghosts

Ø

(Plato knew
what the man was looking for
what the woman was missing

wrote the myth
so we'd remember)

Ø

tillable soil
striped by
clay-piped
ditches
browed with brown cattails
& bruises of lupine

how I loved the wild
asparagus
tiger lilies &
black-eyed susans
beside the culvert

& its tiny salt-less sea
brimming with snails
& stone teeth

Ø

Burn
what's dead in spring
so greenness
can come in

The new is
always a chore

Ø

INLAND's a reedy pond
hand-dug & hand-sewn

its catfish drowning
its color
        drains
the fabric
thins

Ø

You can drive there, I say
meaning *I* could

I can point my nose
anywhere INLAND & go

The cars rise from their haunches
   to daily exhaust & foul the roads

& the roads themselves
   are arrow-straight stays
in the corset of INLAND

      with its stricture of county
& seat full of judges
         beside the white
      Corinthian columns

(all borrowed
except the geography
& history
         of the used-to-be sea)

            Ø

INLAND
prisons abound

all around it
is everything
that's real & alive!

            climate
& industry culture &
philosophy every
letter ever sown &
thought that could
be known

the weight of what
surrounds it grows

how much can it bear?

Ø

INLAND is everybody
the same everywhere

euchre & recipes

Would you bake me a cake? you ask
I would darn your socks
& cut your hair

we would ferment there
be each other's
well-aged wine—

It's enough? you venture

No
It's a god-awful bore

Throw off the covers
get out of bed

(INLAND I am
wherever we are)

See, we're almost there!

Ø

You know we're always talking
about more than one thing, I say

Yeah, I know, you say

            Wait, what are they?
  I mean, what's the other one?

            Ø

INLAND we make trinkets
for tourists to buy

   they want to show they have visited
they want to believe they've been here

Nest algae
        no, Nostalgia

            Ø

Inside INLAND
   it's wild

        & desolate
   as the open sea

an unmet shore
of roving grief

           monstrous
        with fossils
        and cicadas

                Ø

INLAND is slow & stormy
  undefended   uncountried

    filled with the sadness
      of the unaffiliated

such is the learning
            that happens
      in the absence
of question

the walk of the sleepers
whose feet meet
no tension
        of ground

oh how it echoes

                Ø

But, seriously,
            what's in there? you ask

You want me to tell you
  a story of INLAND?

It happened one morning
                    at the edge
  of the neighbor's hayfield

    an Eagle leapt from the
                    top of a dying pine
        whipped out wings
      the span of a tractor a baler a rake

& swooped down
      to a bed of fawns
    snatching one up
in its yellow talons—

    the Doe bellowed & bawled
drove her hooves into the Eagle's load

 What else could she do?

    the Eagle struggled to rise
with its speckled breakfast

    but the Doe would not relent
she won the body back

& it lay— is there still—
  bleeding
              into the field

Continent

Ragged-edged remnant
　　of what once was whole

　　　　river and bandaged
　　with rivers and ranges

violent beginnings
　　that echo still

Consisting of a crust
　as in a pie or a scab

　　with (more)
　　　　and (other)
　　　　　below

　Lift its lithosphere
as you would
the lid of a chest
　(Pandora's/treasure)

inside its childhood
you'll find the mechanics
　of beginnings ocean
sperm washing machine
　toe-bone-connected-
　　　　to-the-foot-bone
　　　crocks of fat and jars of honey
　　hard-boiled eggs   neon tennis ball
hypodermic needle and embroidery thread
　　　　　　a mystifying navel string
　　　　the blue moldy roots
　　　　of everything

The body of Continent
behaves with elasticity
and breeds synchronicity

(nearly always one syllable
more than you thought one
layer   one mile more)

   but when the fault line parts
      like fender from car
  uprises the layered
     inner geography

driving into the day
    fox den and headlight
tubes   battery   graveyard spurge

liquid earth wobbles down its highway
       in weary orbit

   and *hang on*—

   this tectonic bed
  we share its floods
  twisters fires quakes

    roomy enough
for shelves and plates
younger mobile belts
(Himalayas and Urals)

round and around
  it goes   slippery
    magnets on a
  spinning planet!

Continent because
we need a container
for the gorges and falls

When I was a child
I dreamt the Continent
filled with creatures

　　Wild among the wild
　　　　I rode on crustal rafts
　　above the molten core

Soon I learned the mineral self
the heavy sediment *o do not stir*
cerium erbium thulium ytterbium

　　settlements of sediment
　　　　　　rare rare earth
　　what elements I'm made of

　　　　　this restless matter of mine
　　　　I now conserve

　　　　Continent is
that which hangs together
retaining the shape of its origin

　　　a netted whole
　　　with a beating heart
　　　newborn in my arms

One night I saw a human figure
          on a piece of paper

      I felt its eruption
    of spirit cartwheel

Look! I!
          I am!
a whole being
within a blank sea

          color, pattern—
          it made itself
          known to me

      Can a Continent
      demand regard?

      A manuscript once
      appeared as many
    multi-colored squares
              pierced in the middle
              with yarn

I fitted the pieces together
          this way & that
    they began to accumulate
      to cover my body my bed

      they were green & yellow fields
    below my wing   walled cities
    nation states   principalities
      the whole partitioned
          political earth!

Some days I eat Continent
its ginger   mushrooms
rosemary and salt

Day unto day I examine it probe its contours

its soft hills   the places   where it bends

where it opens   its hungry regions and

mossy passages   I want it to   surprise me

I believe possibility dwells within its rifts

and escarpment something in there making

new an immensity that will   not   diminish

Notes

"Full sail…" is from *Metamorphoses* by Ovid, translated by Rolfe Humphries, 1955; the line breaks are mine.

"I am the shore…" is from a poem by Dejan Stojanović, a Serbian writer; it was published in *The Shape* (New Avenue Books, 2012), the English translation of *Oblik* (Gramatik, Podgorica, 2000).

"Love is a shore" by Hilary Sallick, an American poet, first appeared in *The Inflectionist Review* and is the title poem of her book (Lily Poetry Review Books, 2023).

"Seaway"

what is created by humans/ is almost always alien is from Fanny Howe.

fulness of time is from Galatians 4:4, King James Version.

"Peninsula"

In the third section, the text is excerpted from a lecture on bees by Rudolf Steiner at the Goetheanum in Dornach, Switzerland; February 3, 1923.

Schopenhauer believed in a "substratum of all appearances," which he called the *thing-in-itself.*

A semi-colon tattoo is a symbol of mental health awareness; it demonstrates continuation with a new beginning as opposed to the finality of a period.

The notion of 'unmoored speculative futurism' comes from a blog post about bees and posthumanism by Daksha Madhu Rajagopalan, in the online journal, *EnviroSociety.*

"Archipelago"

What you seek is what you find because it is already in you as an image is from Fanny Howe, *The Winter Sun*.

"Strait"

Dirk Keppel, a Civil War soldier, ended a letter to his brother with these words: *Brother, I have to stop writing because the page is only getting smaller and I remain.*

The line, *All straits, and none but straits,* is from John Donne's poem, "Hymn to God, My God, in My Sickness."

The Mystic River in Massachusetts was known by local indigineous people as the "MissiTuk," meaning "great tidal river;" in the 19th century, clipper ships were built on its banks and sailed out to the ocean; it was dammed in 1966.

"Continent"

Day unto day is found in Psalm 19, King James Version, and is also the title of a book of poetry by Martha Collins.

Acknowledgements

Grateful acknowledgment is due to the editors of the following publications where these sequences, some in earlier versions, first appeared:

Another Chicago Magazine: "Archipelago"
Lily Poetry Review: "(INLAND)"
Oxidant | Engine Box Set Vol. 4: "Peninsula"
River Heron Review : "Continent"
Sugar House Review: "Seaway"
The Lincoln Review: "Strait"

Best of the Net nomination, "Continent"
Pushcart Prize nomination: "Strait"

My work has been enriched by so many teachers over the years, including Cindy Ballenger and Jack LeVert, Susan Donnelley, the late John VandeZande, Philip Legler, and Harold Bond. The Joiner Center for the Study of War and Social Consequences was also a place of deep learning for me; my thanks to Afaa Weaver, Bruce Weigl, Marilyn Nelson, Martha Collins, Martín Espada, Brian Turner, Danielle Legros Georges, John Dean, and others.

These poems have benefited from the insights of many, including Linda Haviland Conte, provider of tea and chocolate, and members of the New England Poetry Club workshop, and Bert Stern and Tam Neville's Monday night workshop. I am especially grateful to Hilary Sallick for her friendship and steadfast encouragement, for her keen eye and ear, and for her example of care and attention. I could ask for no better friend and reader.

My thanks to Eileen Cleary for championing my work and to Martha McCollough for the beauty of its presentation. It gives me special joy to have my brother Steve's watercolor on the cover.

My sons, Liam and Kai, keep me going; Coulier, Dunya, and Dover are my daily companions. My love, Steve Bodwell, is the nurturer who makes my writing life possible.

Author Bio

photo: Stephen Bodwell

Mary Buchinger is the author of seven collections of poetry, including *Navigating the Reach* (Salmon Poetry, 2023), *Virology* (Lily Poetry Review Books, 2022), /klaʊdz/ (Lily Poetry Review Books, 2021), einfühlung/*in feeling* (Main Street Rag, 2018), *Aerialist* (Gold Wake, 2015; May Swenson Poetry Award finalist, *The Journal*/Wheeler Prize semifinalist, Perugia Press Prize semifinalist). She has received poetry awards from the New England Poetry Club and the Virginia Poetry Society, a Norton Island Residency, and over a dozen Pushcart Prize and Best of the Net nominations. Her poetry appears in *AGNI, Gargoyle, Hollins Critic, Laurel Review, Lincoln Review, Nimrod, On the Seawall, Plume, Salt Hill, Seneca Review, South Dakota Review, Sugar House Review, Queen Mob's Teahouse,* and elsewhere. She teaches at the Massachusetts College of Pharmacy and Health Sciences in Boston and serves on the board of the New England Poetry Club.

www.MaryBuchinger.com